A GREEN WORLD?

Nicola Baird

W

FRANKLIN WATTS

LONDON•SYDNEY

Revised and updated 2004

Franklin Watts
96 Leonard Street,
London EC2A 4XD

Franklin Watts Australia
45–51 Huntley Street
Alexandria
NSW 2015

© Franklin Watts 1997, 2004

Text update: Andrea Smith
Editor: Matthew Parselle
Series editor: Rachel Cooke
Designer: John Christopher & Helen White, White Design
Series designer: Nigel Soper, Millions Design
Picture research: Susan Mennell

A CIP catalogue record for this book
is available from the British Library.

ISBN 0 7496 5350 7

Dewey Classification 363.7
Printed in Malaysia

Picture credits (b=bottom; t=top; r=right; l=left; c=centre):
Body Shop International Plc: p. 21t; Bruce Coleman: p. 8 tl (Mark Boulton), 25b (Staffan Widstrand); Corbis/Bettmann/UPI: p. 8tr, Brooks Kraft 25t; Sue Cunningham Photographic: p. 19c; Ecoscene: p. 10t, 11t, 20b (Nick Hawkes); Ronald Grant Archive/MGM/Pathe Communications: p. 19b; Popperfoto: p. 11b, 13b (Alan Greeley), 15b (Alexander Joe/AFP), 19t (Will Burgess), 20t (Peter Benchley), 21b (Kevin Harvey), 23t, 29b; Rex Features: p. 26, 27c; Still Pictures: p. 4t (DRA), 4b (EIA), 5t (Ray Pfortner), 5b (Mark Edwards), 6t (Al Grillo), 6b (Dylan Garcia), 7t (Herbert Giradet), 7b (Harmut Schwarzbach), 8-9 (Andre Maslenniker), 9t (Harmut Schwarzbach), 10b (Mark Edwards), 12t (Andre Bartschi), 12b (Roland Seitre), 13t (Nigel Dickinson), 14t and b (Mark Edwards), 15t (B & C Alexander), 16t (Mark Edwards), 16b (Paul Harrison), 17t (Mark Edwards), 17b and 18t (Harmut Schwarzbach), 18b (John Maier), 22t (David Drain), 22b (Martin Wright), 23b (David J Cross), 24t (Adrian Arbib), 27b (Mark Edwards), 28tl (B & C Alexander), 28tr (Thomas Raupach), 29t (Carlos Guarita/ Reportage).

Quotation credits, given from the top of a page beginning with the left-hand column: p. 5 1 Prince Charles, keynote address to World Commission on Environment and Development, 22 April, 1992; 2 Paul Hawken, The Ecology of Commerce; 3 Gustavo Krause, former minister of the environment, *The Times*, 9 December, 1996 p. 6 1 E F Schumacher, Small is Beautiful, 1993; 2 J Davis, *Scientific American*, September, 1950 p. 7 1 Greenpeace report, 1996 p. 8 Hilary French, Worldwatch, 1990 p. 9 1 *Ecos*, Issue 16, 1995; 2 Global Climate Coalition 2001; 3 Mark Johnston, Friends of the Earth, 2001 p. 11 1 World Resources, 1992-93; 2 Statement from the Green Market Development Group at www.thegreenpowergroup.org, 19:9:03; 3 Fred Pearce, *New Scientist*, 20 July, 1996; 4 Worldwatch, 2003; p. 12 United Nations Environment Programme, Global Biodiversity Assessment, 1995 p. 13 1 C Mann and M Plummer, theme within Noah's Choice: The Future of Endangered Species, 1995; 2 James Fairhead and Melissa Reach, Institute of Development Studies, University of Sussex, *Independent on Sunday*, 1 December, 1996; 3 David Bellamy, botanist, Blooming Bellamy: Herbs and Healing, 1993; 4 www.buckscc.gov.uk/countryside/biodiversity/biodiversity_action _plan/habitat11.stm p. 14 Fox Qwaina, secondary school headmaster, *Link*, November/December, 1996 p. 15 1 Anne Boston, *Country Living*, September, 1996; 2 Institute of Food Science & Technology, www.ifst.org p. 16 1 Paul Ehrlich, scientist, The Population Timebomb, 1968; 2 Boutros Boutros-Ghali, Secretary General, United Nations, 1994 p. 17 1 World Resources 1992-93; 2 Caring for the Earth: A Strategy for Sustainable Living, Earthscan, 1991 p. 18 1 Emrys Jones, Metropolis: The World's Great Cities, 1990; 2 Marcus Colchester and Larry Lohmann, The Struggle for Land and the Fate of the Forests, 1993 p. 19 1 John Houghton, Global Warming, 1994; 2 Professor John Whitelegg, Professor of Environmental Studies, Liverpool John Moores University, *Transport Retort*, January/February, 1997 p. 20 Andy Coghlan, *New Scientist* p. 21 1 Alan Knight, environmental manager, B&Q, 1994; 2 David Bellamy, botanist, *The Observer*, September, 1996; 3 Anita Roddick, Body and Soul, 1991; 4 Antonia Johnson, chairwoman of Axel Johnson AB p. 22 1 WasteWatch, 2001; 2 *The Economist*, 29 May, 1993 p. 23 1 Michael Jacobs, economist, The Green Economy, 1991; 2 Ron Kaplan, The Environmental Magazine posted at www.enn.com/ news/2003-06-25/s_4811.asp; 3 US Congress Office of Technology Assessment, Serious Reduction of Hazardous Waste, 1986 p. 25 1 Martin Khor Kok Peng, director, Third World Network, 1992; 2 Agenda 21, 1992; 3 John Naisbitt, Global Paradox, 1995 p. 26 1 Marchioness of Worcester, actress, *Daily Telegraph*, 9 February 1996; 2 AA spokesman, *The Guardian*, 8 August, 1996; 3 *Utne Reader*, July/August, 1992 p. 27 Tony Juniper, executive director, Friends of the Earth, *The Times*, 14 February, 1996 p. 28 1 George Kennan, *Foreign Affairs*, Issue 48, 1970; 2 Friends of the Earth, www.foei.org/publications p. 29 1 Simon Schooner, Canadian Nuxalk elder, June, 1996; 2 Michael Jacobs, economist, The Green Economy, 1991; 3 John Naisbitt, Global Paradox, 1995; 4 Maurice Strong, Secretary General, UNCED, June, 1992

Thanks to Isabelle Cooper and Angharad Beurle-Williams

Contents

A green world?

We often use the word 'green' to describe something which is environmentally friendly or someone who is an environmentalist. But what exactly do we mean by the 'environment'? Dictionaries often describe it in very general terms as 'external surroundings'. Even in law, the term 'environment' does not have a precise meaning – in fact, the oldest environmental laws refer only to plants and animals. Some environmental campaigners concern themselves with one particular issue such as saving whales or recycling waste. However, the word environment is often used in a much wider sense to describe the world around us.

▲ *Many people are concerned about the damage we are causing to our home, planet Earth.*

◀ *Saving whales from slaughter is just one issue that environmentalists campaign for.*

Most aspects of the environment are interlinked in some way and many of the problems with it are caused by economic development. Feeding the world's growing population, for example, is one of the biggest problems we face. To try to solve it, many governments

Many business people welcome the idea of sustainable development. They see it as a method to guarantee responsible, well-managed economic growth which will ensure a healthy world environment for the future.

66 *We have the ability to recreate a remarkably different economy, one that can restore and protect the environment while bringing prosperity, meaningful work, and true security.* 99
Paul Hawken, The Ecology of Commerce

But the balance between preserving the natural environment and allowing industry to grow can be difficult to find – especially if companies are reluctant to cooperate. Many people have criticized businesses for ignoring the idea of sustainable development and carrying on with their business as usual, with little regard for the environment.

▲ *Some people blame industry for many environmental problems, including pollution.*

encourage farmers to use chemicals and fertilizers to get bigger harvests. However, this can also damage the land, making it more difficult to grow crops and, therefore, more difficult to feed the poor and hungry.

66 *We will not protect the environment until we address the issue of population growth and poverty in the same breath.* 99
Prince Charles at the World Commission on Environment and Development

It is because environmental problems can spoil the quality of life for everyone and everything that an idea called 'sustainable development' has become important. Sustainable development means having a growing and healthy economy which meets our present needs but one which also does not spoil the planet or the ability of future generations to meet their needs.

▼ *The 'Tree of Life' at the Earth Summit meeting in Rio, Brazil. This meeting aimed to solve the problems of the environment through the idea of sustainable development.*

66 *The question now is how to introduce economic activities that are sustainable from an environmental point of view. Is the environment the limit or the opportunity? Is it on a collision course with the economy, or is it a new path?* 99
Gustavo Krause, Brazil's Minister of the Environment (1995–98)

However, people all over the world are still trying to find the solutions to the problems that affect us all. In this book we look at whether we can have a green world at the same time as a healthy economy.

Green power?

However, some people do not see our use of fossil fuels as a problem. Some economists claim fossil fuels will not run out because, as with any other substance, when they become rare their price will go up – so businesses will be forced to look for and use cheaper alternatives. Many businesses also take this line.

66 *If allowed to pursue 'business as usual', energy industries can supply us with all that is necessary to power industrial civilization far into the future.* **99**
J Davis, Scientific American journal

Around 95 per cent of the energy used by businesses comes from 'fossil fuels' – such as oil, coal and natural gas – which are provided by the Earth's natural resources. There are two fundamental problems with using fossil fuels. Firstly, they release gases which pollute the atmosphere and cause global warming as we will see in later chapters. The second problem is that they cannot be reused – they are not sustainable – and many people believe that, eventually, they will run out.

66 *Fossil fuels are not made by men; they cannot be recycled. Once they are gone they are gone for ever.* **99**
E F Schumacher, Small is Beautiful

▶ *Another oil problem is the damage from spills. The Prestige lost 64,000 tons in 2002.*

▼ *Nuclear energy is an alternative to fossil fuels. Its proponents see it as a clean, safe and efficient option.*

But many people believe that we must use less fossil fuels and more alternative energy sources to curb global warming. Options include tree and crop waste (already widely used), harnessing the power of wind and waves, trapping heat naturally produced deep underground (geothermal energy) or using the energy of falling water (hydroelectric power). The Sun is another huge untapped energy resource.

These wind turbines generate electricity without releasing pollutants into the air. Denmark, Germany and Spain installed 78 per cent of all the new wind power added worldwide in 2002.

66 *In half an hour enough of the Sun's energy is received by Earth to power humankind's activities for a year. The amount of sunlight which falls on buildings in the UK could supply two-thirds of all our electricity needs.* **99**
Greenpeace report

Some countries see solar power as an effective and commercially viable energy source. For example, Japan's Sunshine Project aims to have 70,000 houses fitted with solar panels by 2005; the Netherlands wants 100,000 homes fitted with solar panels by 2010. The World Solar Energy Programme, launched in Zimbabwe in 1996, hopes to provide solar power to light classrooms, irrigate fields and provide water pumps, cookers and fridges in more than 60 countries.

The shower is attached to panels that use the energy of the Sun to heat the water. Even in a cloudy country like Britain, this system can be used to provide hot water.

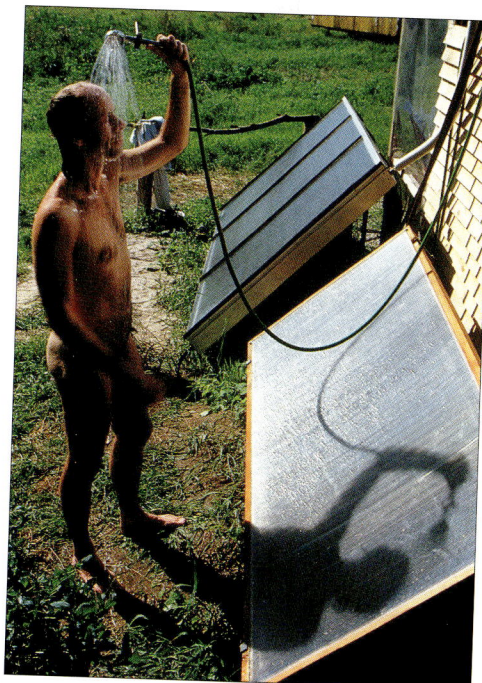

However, these energy sources do not always produce electricity when it is needed. Some way has to be found of storing it. Hydrogen fuel is one possible solutation. Renewable energy can be used to fuel the production of easily-stored hydrogen liquid or gas. It, in turn, powers fuel cells that generate electricity through a chemical reaction – the combination of hydrogen and oxygen to make water. Iceland intends to switch from fossil fuels to hydrogen by 2040, using geothermal and hydroelectric energy to power the manufacture of hydrogen.
But today renewable energies still only provide a fraction of our power. In 2000, wind power generated just 0.1 per cent of the USA's electricity.

Polluter pays?

Pollution comes from people – from our industries, like power stations and chemical factories, to our car exhaust fumes and our sewage. Pollution adds to global warming problems and can spoil the quality of people's life.

❝ *In Hungary, the government attributes one in 17 deaths to air pollution. In Bombay breathing the air is equivalent to smoking 10 cigarettes a day. And in Beijing air pollution-related respiratory disease is so common that it has been dubbed the 'Beijing cough'.* ❞
Hilary French, Worldwatch

Back in 1963 Rachel Carson shocked the world with her book *Silent Spring* which described the damaging effect chemical pollutants, such as DDT, can have on the environment and the food chain. Although she changed the views of many Americans about pesticides, even now farmers still use such chemicals on their crops to increase the likelihood of big harvests.

Many people are also concerned about the relatively unknown but potentially dangerous effects of working with nuclear energy and storing nuclear waste. Despite claims from the nuclear industry that it is cleaner and safer than traditional power plants, some people see nuclear accidents (like

▲ A helicopter spraying crops. Chemicals are widely used in modern farming methods.

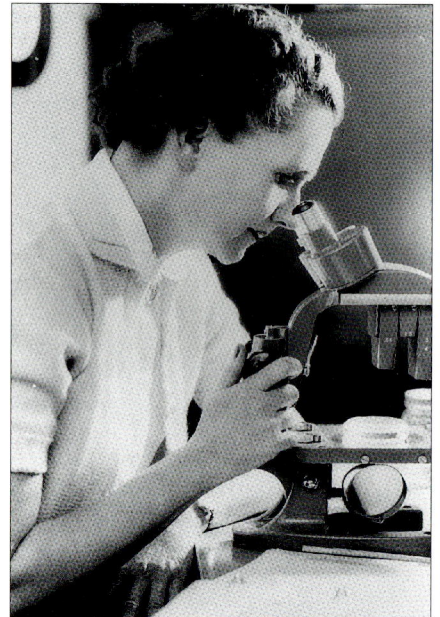

▲ US author and scientist Rachel Carson criticized the use of chemical pollutants.

those at Three Mile Island and Chernobyl) and problems associated with nuclear waste storage as the greatest pollution threat for future generations.

But can we reduce pollution and its bad effects while, at the same time, continuing to enjoy the benefits of a thriving economy? Some people would say yes – as long as the commitment to a cleaner and safer environment is there.

66 It is possible to reduce pollution ... it has to be paid for.... What the public is prepared to pay for depends on how far it understands and supports the need for it. 99
Ecos, Environmental publication

▶ Cities, such as Shanghai in China, are often affected by the smog which pollution produces.

▼ Acid rain, which is caused by pollution, can have a damaging effect. These trees in Poland have been destroyed by acid rain.

Many people believe that there should be stricter anti-pollution laws. However, some businesses in countries where laws are already tougher complain that this puts them at a disadvantage compared to businesses in countries where legislation is lax. They say that the cost of putting in cleaner technology allows businesses from nations with less strict legislation to under-cut their prices. This may mean that they lose customers, profits and jobs. As a result, industry often prefers voluntary agreements to use greener technology.

Some businesses and politicians in industrialized countries do not think that global warming should be tackled through rules like the Kyoto Treaty that require cuts in the greenhouse gases believed to be responsible. The treaty was signed in 1997 by 54 nations. After the US backed out in 2001 because of a weakening economy, a scaled-down version was signed by 180 countries.

66 The Kyoto Treaty has led us down a dead end street. The time has come for a new direction on climate policy based on the ability of businesses to lead the development of new technologies to address global concerns about greenhouse gas emissions. 99
Global Climate Coalition

Preserving the environment is creating new industries. Eighteen wind farms planned for the British coast should supply electricity to more than a million homes and create more than 8,000 jobs.

66 This is the dawn of new era in energy and the beginning of a major new UK industry. 99
Mark Johnston, Friends of the Earth

Global warming?

Even though scientists know the world's climate has changed, it is still unclear exactly what damage is done to the environment by increases in global temperatures. However, climate change (or global warming) could mean drought and food shortages for Africa, the loss of forests, the spread of tropical diseases like malaria, a wetter Britain, and a rise in sea levels which would flood island

▲ Many people enjoy sunbathing, but campaigns warning about skin cancer have persuaded some to either use protective creams or stay in the shade. 'Slip! Slop! Slap!' is one such campaign, used in Australia.

nations such as Kiribati in the South Pacific. The thinning of the ozone layer is another concern. The layer, which protects the Earth from the Sun's harmful ultraviolet rays, is being destroyed, mainly by gases called CFCs. They were banned in 1987, but are long-lasting and are continuing to create two giant holes in the layer over the north and south poles and to cause its depletion over other parts of the world. In Australia, worries about the increasing number of people suffering from skin cancers caused by the Sun's rays, led

to a government campaign entitled 'Slip! Slop! Slap!' which encourages people to use protective sun creams.

There is still some debate about whether or not human activities have any effect on global warming and the ozone hole. Some people believe that the climate is changing naturally – many others would disagree.

"A natural greenhouse effect keeps the earth's surface warm.... Human activities not only increase the atmospheric concentrations of naturally occurring greenhouse gases but also add new powerful gases such as the industrial chemicals known as CFCs."
World Resources

CFCs, once used in most fridges and aerosols sprays, are also thought to contribute to the greenhouse effect as well as damaging the ozone layer. But since a *New York Times* article in 1995 with the heading 'Scientists finally confirm human role in global warming', some effort has been made to cut emissions of greenhouse gases such as carbon dioxide and methane.

"The Green Market Development is a collaboration of 12 leading corporations and the World Resources Institute dedicated to building corporate markets for green power. Our goal is to develop corporate markets for 1,000 megawatts of new, cost competitive green power by 2010."
Green Market Development Group

But despite initiatives like this, many companies are reluctant to make changes to the way they do business. They blame the methods of developing countries, rather than themselves, for environmental problems. However, developing countries see this as just an excuse to stop their economies catching up with those of the richer countries. This can make international negotiations difficult.

▲ Traffic fumes can increase the levels of greenhouse gases in the air, thus adding to the problems of global warming.

"For all the talk of 'sustainable development' ... half the citizens of the rich world sincerely believe that it is poor tropical farmers burning the rainforests, rather than their own fossil-fuel burning, gas-guzzling lifestyles that is causing the greenhouse effect."
Fred Pearce, New Scientist

Solving environmental problems need not necessarily be bad for business. Fridge manufacturers found alternatives for CFCs and some oil companies, such as BP, are at the forefront of introducing renewable energies.

"Annual production of solar power systems has grown 150 per cent in the past three years... Already the cheapest source of power in many remote, off-grid locations, solar cells can help meet the power needs of some of the 2 billion people who now lack access to modern energy services."
Worldwatch Institute, 2003

◀ CFCs were once used in many aerosol sprays, but concerns about the damage they do to the ozone layer have caused them to be banned.

Protecting wildlife?

Life on Earth is amazingly rich and varied. Scientists have named around 1.4 million different types of plant, animal, fish, bird, insect and fungus, although it is estimated that there could be anywhere between 5 to 30 million species. This variety and abundance of life is known as biodiversity.

▶ *These beautifully coloured macaws are just one species out of the millions that live on this planet.*

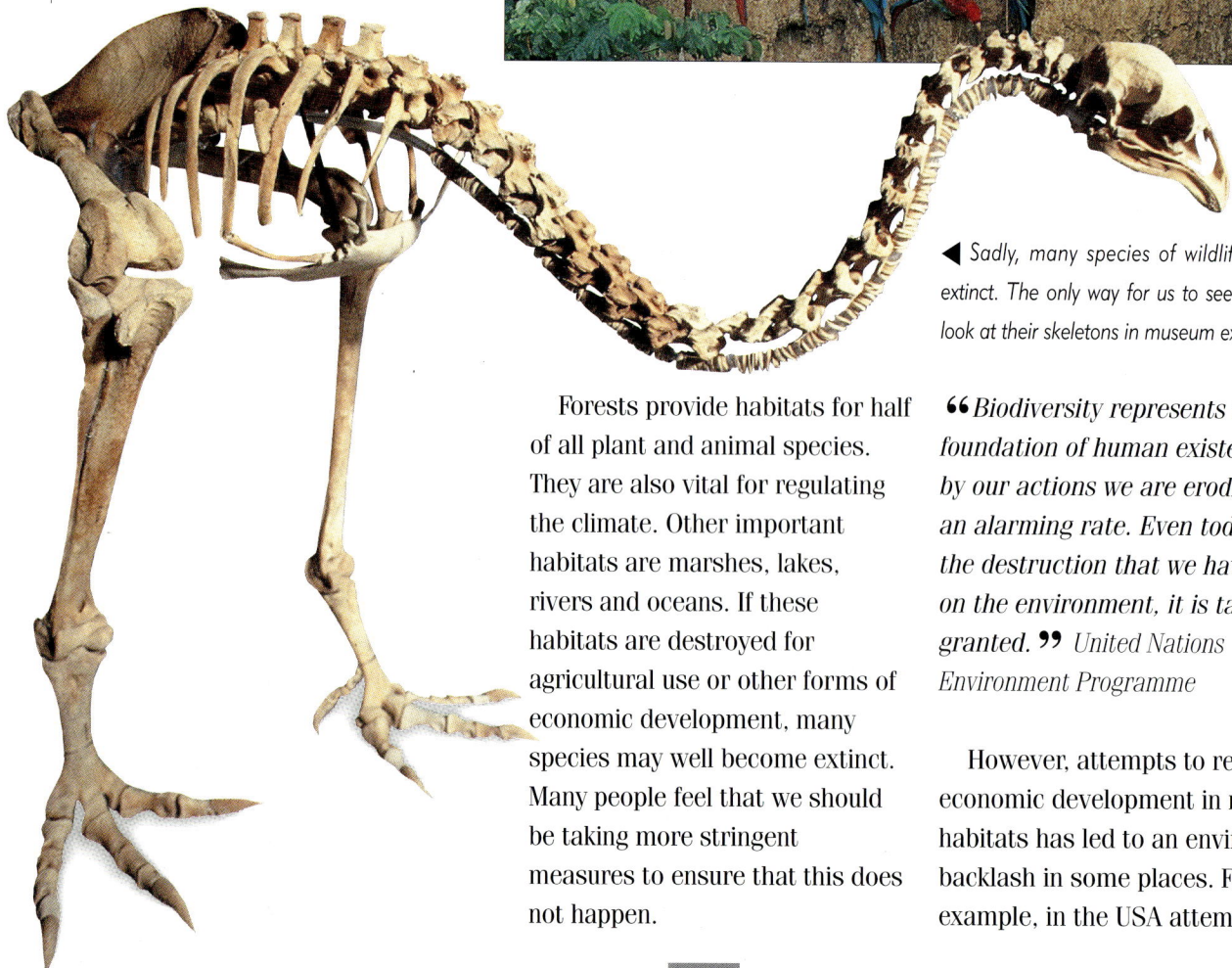

◀ *Sadly, many species of wildlife are now extinct. The only way for us to see them is to look at their skeletons in museum exhibits.*

Forests provide habitats for half of all plant and animal species. They are also vital for regulating the climate. Other important habitats are marshes, lakes, rivers and oceans. If these habitats are destroyed for agricultural use or other forms of economic development, many species may well become extinct. Many people feel that we should be taking more stringent measures to ensure that this does not happen.

" *Biodiversity represents the foundation of human existence. Yet by our actions we are eroding [it] at an alarming rate. Even today, despite the destruction that we have inflicted on the environment, it is taken for granted.* **"** *United Nations Environment Programme*

However, attempts to reduce economic development in natural habitats has led to an environmental backlash in some places. For example, in the USA attempts to preserve a forest where Northern spotted owls nested were criticized by loggers who feared that their jobs were at risk if logging stopped.

66 The Endangered Species Act shows that the [US] government cares more about the well-being of animals no one has ever heard of than it does about human welfare. 99
C Mann and M Plummer, Noah's Choice: The Future of Endangered Species

It is also possible that claims about the destruction of the environment have been exaggerated in some cases.

66 Environmentalists claim that the West African forests have been disappearing fast in the past 40 years, but there is often more forest cover today than a generation ago. 99
Institute of Development Studies, University of Sussex

Despite this, some estimates suggest that 25 per cent of the world's 250,000 species of flowering plant could become extinct over the next 50 years. As many plants have important medical uses – for example, quinine is used to treat malaria and the Madagascan Rosy Periwinkle to treat Hodgkin's disease and childhood leukaemia – it is important to prevent their extinction. The Royal Botanic Gardens at Kew, London, has set up a 'seed bank' to collect and conserve ten per cent, up to 25,000 species, of the world's seed-bearing plants. The collection of UK plants is 97 per cent complete and the project should be finished in 2010.

▲ A Kenyan woman picking Tuba aka – a medicinal plant which can cure fever.

66 Without natural vegetation, and the plants and animals which it supports and which support us, I believe the human race has little chance of survival. 99
David Bellamy, botanist

People who live in rainforests use their natural habitat as a kind of bank too. They use the wood from trees for housing and canoe making. Many plants are used for treating illnesses like headaches, allergies and fevers. Fruit and nut trees are harvested for their delicious crops. Many people see this way of using the materials the environment provides for us in a productive way as one way forward in terms of sustainable economic development. But, as ever, what is truly sustainable is still open to question.

66 The conservation of biodiversity is essentially the same as nature conservation but with a renewed emphasis on the importance of all species... 99 Buckingham and Milton Keynes Biodiversity Action Plan 2000–2010

▼ Kew Gardens aims to increase the number of plants available for human use.

Organic food?

Farming has had a dramatic effect on our environment. For example, clearing forest land to grow soya beans to feed cattle can lead to the extinction of the wildlife that lives there. If the land is cleared by burning trees this will release CO_2 into the atmosphere, adding to the problem of global warming which, in turn, may have a damaging effect on the fertility of the soil. Land is also under pressure from, to give but a few examples, expanding towns and cities, out-of-town shopping centres, landfill sites and growing populations throughout the world today.

▲▼ The Amazon rainforest, Brazil. More than 13 per cent of the Amazon rainforest has been destroyed. Much of it has been cleared to make way for cattle ranches.

The decrease in fertility of farm land has led to farmers looking for new ways of getting bigger harvests. One way to do this is to use agricultural fertilisers. Some European and North American grain farmers put between 100-500 kilograms (kg) of nitrogen a year on a hectare of land compared to Africa where the figure is 5kg per hectare. But relying on such artificial methods may make the soil even less fertile in the long term. It can also be expensive and thereby force farmers into debt. As a result, some people still prefer a more traditional approach.

66 We try to show students simple and cheap ways to grow vegetables using nitrogen-rich beans, which are good for the soil, crop rotation and organic manure. 99
Fox Qwaina, school headmaster, Solomon Islands

However, there are still an enormous number of people going hungry, so governments encourage farmers to use chemicals on their soil to boost crop yield. But more than 100 million people died of hunger during the 1970s. Today there are 815 million people who are undernourished in the world, with 777 million of them in developing regions.

Many people are also concerned about the effects on our health of using fertilizers and pesticides on food crops, or feeding additives and antibiotics to animals which are being bred for their meat. Can all these chemicals really be doing us any good?

◄ The effects of food shortages and malnutrition are all too obvious in this child from a developing country in Africa.

▲ Unfortunately, not all organic food is as cheap as the bread shown here. Many people fear it will remain a luxury available only to the better off.

❝ *I want to be able to eat apples, carrots and potatoes without worrying about pesticides absorbed into the skin ... it seems logical to assume that produce grown without any chemical inputs is safest of all. Arguably it will also taste better.* **❞**
Anne Boston,
Country Living

Health scares may explain why an increasing number of people are buying organic food. This is not genetically-engineered and is grown without the use of artificial fertilisers and pesticides.

❝ *A report by Taylor Nelson/Sofres (2002) indicated that in 2001 79 per cent of UK households made an organic purchase...* **❞** The Institute of Food Science & Technology

Organic food is more expensive though. UK shoppers pay 25 per cent more on average for organic goods, partly because much of it is imported. Environmentalists argue that governments should encourage organic growing so that prices fall.

Organic farming also helps wildlife. Surveys have found 57 per cent more species of wild plants on organic farms, three times as many butterflies and 44 per cent more birds.

Population explosion?

*T*he streets seemed alive with people. People eating, people washing, people sleeping, people visiting, arguing and screaming. People thrusting their hands through the taxi window begging.... People, people, people ... a hellish aspect. **"**
Paul Ehrlich, The Population Timebomb

There are more than 6.3 billion people in the world today and we create an enormous drain on its resources. Every year this number grows by 100 million. Most of this increase occurs in countries that are not industrialized. The Indian subcontinent, for example, adds 21 million people a year, equivalent to the population of Australia. Families in these countries tend to have more children because fewer survive into adulthood. Another reason is that in some countries even very young children are a form of 'wealth' as they can help with daily tasks, like herding goats and collecting firewood. When they grow up they help to farm crops and earn money for family needs. They can also look after their elderly parents.

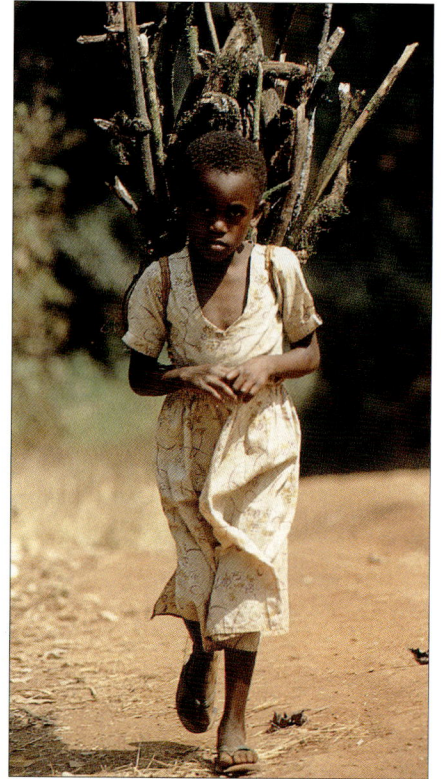

▶ *In many developing countries children are often used as free labour. This Cameroonian child is collecting firewood to take home.*

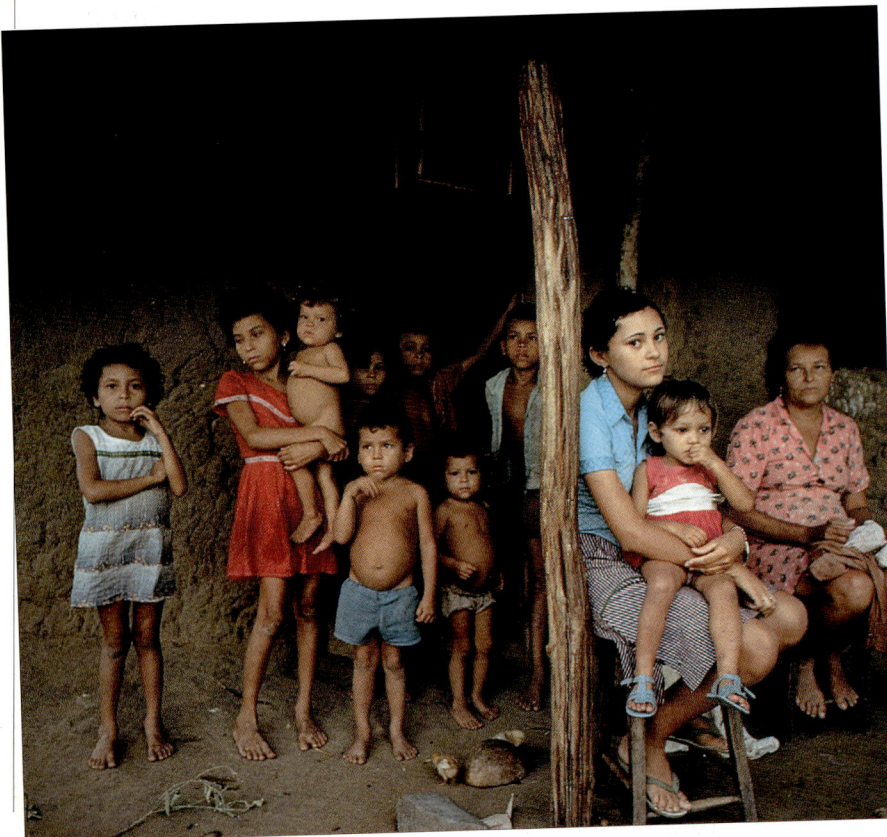

"*Children are among the first victims ... of environmental degradation. In all countries of the world, rich and poor, they are the first to suffer from poverty, malnutrition, disease and pollution.* **"**
Boutros Boutros-Ghali, former Secretary General of the United Nations

◀ *Mlosa Lopes de Souza, a 35-year-old Brazilian woman, is pictured here with ten of her fourteen living children. Her religion forbids the use of contraception. Families of this size are not uncommon in the developing world.*

For sustainable development to work should we be thinking about moving away from the throwaway, consumer society in which we live? Or should we be looking at ways to reduce population growth? Some believe a combination of the two factors is the answer.

Living sustainably must be a guiding principle for all the world's people, but it never will be while hundreds of millions live without enough of even the basic essentials of life.... To live within the Earth's limits ... two things will need to be done: population growth must stop everywhere, and the rich must stabilize, and in some cases, reduce, their consumption of resources. Caring for the Earth: A Strategy for Sustainable Living, Earthscan

▲ *This large shopping centre is a good illustration of the level of consumerism in the Western world. Many people now believe that we should try to cut down on the number of things we buy and use.*

Some countries have tried to restrict population growth by law. In China, for example, couples in cities are only allowed to have one child. However, it would be impossible to place such restrictions on everyone as many religions forbid the use of contraception and abortion. Some see family planning as an infringement of basic human rights.

But is the population explosion the reason for the world's dwindling resources? Is the real problem the high consumption rate of products by richer countries compared to that of poorer nations?

▶ *A one-child family in China. China has the biggest population of any country in the world with the result that the government forbids families to have more than one child.*

Green cities, green roads?

Bangkok in Thailand is just one of many cities that are overpopulated, with the result that its roads are often choked with traffic and pollution.

Despite this, cities can be environmentally friendly places. For example Curitiba, in Brazil, recycles 70 per cent of its waste and has increased the amount of green space per person ten-fold. It has also attempted to cut down on levels of traffic pollution by introducing a metro system and a bicycle lane.

However, cities like Curitiba are usually the exception rather than the rule, particularly with regard to road transport. Worldwide, more than 750 million vehicles were in use in 2003, and by 2030 this number could swell

These Brazilian children have been forced to sleep on the street due to overcrowding. Here, they watch the televisions in a shop window.

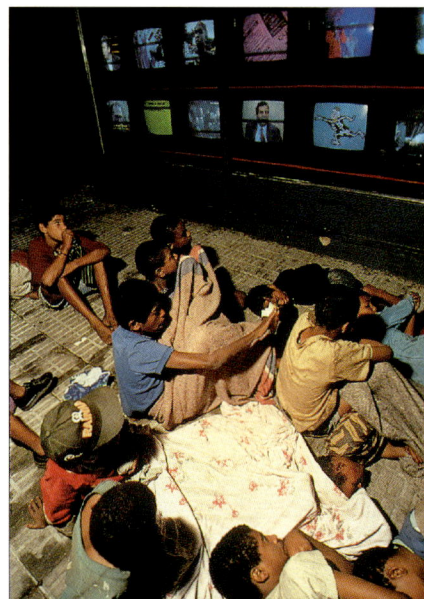

" *No one has driven at snail's pace through London, already late for an appointment and with no guarantee of a parking place at journey's end, without cursing the road system; no one has approached Caracas or Rio through the awfulness of their shanty towns without wondering why they are tolerated; or seen the street-sleepers in Calcutta – or those under Charing Cross Bridge, for that matter – without being convinced that man has made his own hell.* **"**
Emrys Jones, Metropolis: The World's Greatest Cities

Cities cover 2 per cent of the world's surface but use 75 per cent of its resources and produce about the same percentage of its waste. Already about 50 per cent of the world's population lives in cities. In the developing world, people often move to cities because of problems where they live, such as crop failures, lack of grazing land for animals or water shortages. On arrival in a city, many are forced to live in slums with no running water, cookers, sewage services or security. Squatters are at risk of being moved on by the police. Many people see such problems as a great threat to the environment.

" *Local people must be allowed to regain control over their land and economies ... if the twin problems of poverty and environmental destruction are to be tackled.* **"**
Marcus Colchester and Larry Lohmann, The Struggle for Land and The Fate of the Forests

to 1 billion. People like cars, not just for their practical uses, but also for their image which is often associated with status and style. Many 'road' movies, such as *Thelma & Louise*, are often among the top-earning films. But in a recent survey in Hertfordshire, England, only half of those questioned recognized that many environmental and health problems, like asthma, were caused by traffic fumes.

" *Since the 1950s there has been a phenomenal growth in road transport, especially in industrialized countries where road transport now accounts for over 80 per cent of all transport and for nearly 50 per cent of oil consumption.* **"**
John Houghton, Global Warming

Roads can be of great practical use. For example, a basic access track can enable people living in rural areas to travel easily to towns where they can sell their produce. But roads are also criticized for the destruction they can cause. They open up isolated areas like forests and cut through agricultural land destroying habitats for wildlife, indigenous people's traditional lifestyles and peaceful places for leisure activities.

▶ *Cycle rickshaws are a more environmentally friendly alternative to cars.*

▼ *Public transport is often under-funded compared to roads but it can be very efficient.*

However, some people argue that more roads or restrictions are needed because of the increasing levels of traffic, especially in cities. For example, a £5 'congestion charge' was introduced in London in 2003 for vehicles entering the city centre. The success of the scheme has prompted 35 other British cities to consider doing the same. And many nations including France and the US have constructed toll roads and bridges.

" *Why should the Indian government have the slightest interest or respect for sustainability arguments when our comfort and smugness have been built on burning fossil fuels and mass motorization?* **"**
John Whitelegg, Professor of Environmental Studies, Liverpool John Moores University

◀ *The enormously popular Thelma & Louise was just one of many films that has glamorized the image of the car.*

Green shopping?

When France tested nuclear weapons in 1995 in the South Pacific region, some anti-nuclear and environmental campaigners suggested shoppers should stop buying, or boycott, French wine. The aim was to bring attention to the problem by making a significant dent in France's economy. Boycott shopping is often used as a means of protesting against products which in some way harm the environment. It can also encourage companies to stop stocking such products. However, boycott shopping needs to be on a national scale to have any effect at all and this can be very difficult to organize – especially if commitment is lacking.

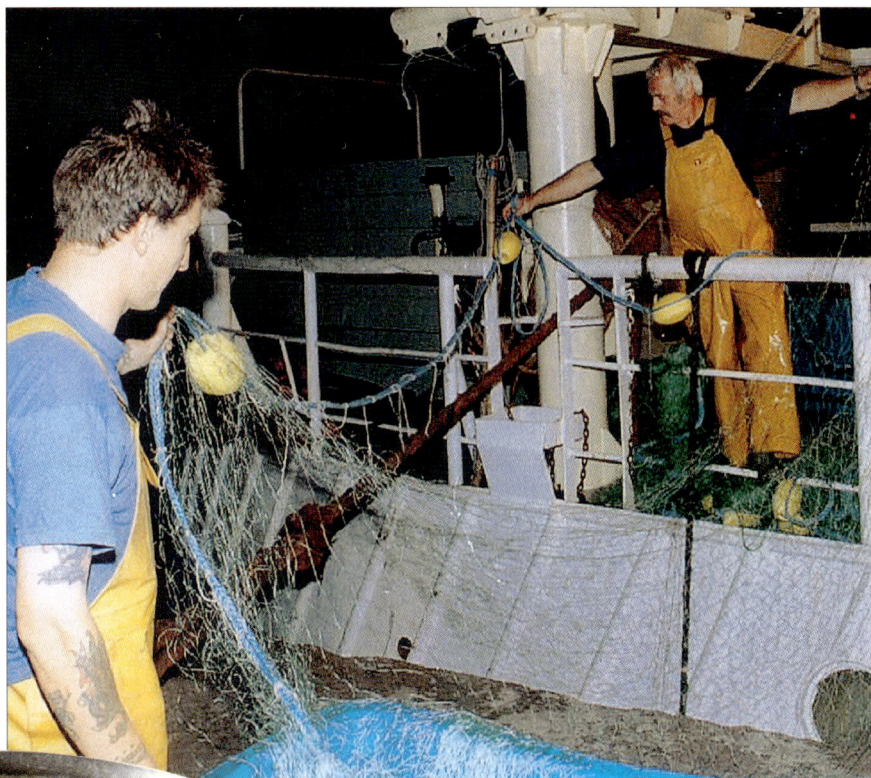

◀▲ The nets used for catching tuna fish have been criticized because other creatures, such as dolphins, can get trapped in them and die. This has led many to boycott tuna caught in this way and turn to more environmentally friendly brands.

APPROVED
dolphin friendly
authorised by the
Whale and Dolphin
Conservation Society

Packed for:
GLENRYCK (UK) LTD
P.O. BOX 22
5 FRIDAY STREET
HENLEY-ON-THAMES
OXON RG9 1AH
PRODUCT OF SEYCHELLES
INGREDIENTS: SOLID PACK
SKIPJACK TUNA
VEGETABLE OIL, SALT

GLENRYCK
SKIPJACK
TUNA STEAKS
IN VEGETABLE OIL

200g 7oz

"Hardcore 'greens' are the only consumers who stick to their guns when it comes to boycotting ethically dubious foods. Outside this extremely committed core of individuals, most boycotters who claim to be green relapse into their former buying habits once an issue fades from the headlines. "
Andy Coghlan, New Scientist

But many people do consider themselves to be environmentally aware and, given the opportunity, would prefer to buy green products.

❝ *None of our customers say they want to buy goods from trashed forests.* **❞**
Alan Knight, Environmental Manager, major DIY chain

This could be done by labelling green products in a way that is easy for consumers to identify. This has already taken place with, for example, 'dolphin-friendly' tuna. But there are still many labels being used which incorrectly claim that a product is environmentally friendly.

❝ *New or expanded power plants can only be labelled as green if the hydropower facility leads to a substantial improvement of the local and regional ecological quality, in excess of the legal compliance.* **❞**
EUGENE, European Green Electricity Network

One way to avoid this would be for shops to stock only products which have passed an inspection by an independent body to make sure that they really are green. This already happens with the Mexico-based Forest Stewardship Council. It assesses if forests are well-managed and timber products from woods that meet its criteria can carry the FSC logo. Worldwide 3.6 per cent of forests used to produce timber are FSC-certified and in the UK this figure is as high as 65 per cent.

Despite this, there is still a question mark over the motives

▲ *Many people want to buy products that are environmentally friendly. However, they often do not have the choice or they are misled by inaccurate labelling. One example of a truly 'green' place to shop is The Body Shop which sells health and beauty products.*

▼ *Anita Roddick, founder of The Body Shop International, is committed to a green policy for her chain of shops. Any item bought from The Body Shop is guaranteed to have been produced without damaging or exploiting local lands or people.*

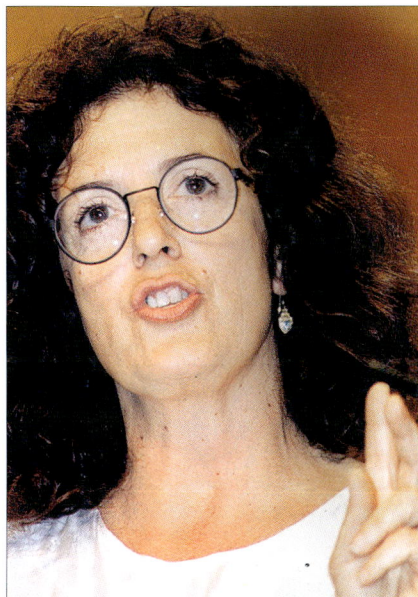

behind some companies' decisions to manufacture green products.

❝ *Many companies are now fighting to clamber aboard the green bandwagon and shouting about their brand new, shining green products and policies. I would be happier if I thought they were motivated by real concern for the environment rather than a desire to increase sales.* **❞**
Anita Roddick, founder of The Body Shop International

Even if some companies are cynical about the environment, many people feel that green shopping is a way to keep both the economy and the environment healthy.

❝ *A store can become an exhibition hall for conveying the concept of sustainable development at a very down-to-earth level.* **❞**
Antonia Johnson, chairwoman Axel Johnson AB, Swedish engineering company

Does recycling work?

One disadvantage of modern consumerism is the amount of waste produced.

66 We produce around 28 million tonnes of household waste in the UK every year. In just one hour we produce enough waste to fill the Albert Hall. 99 WasteWatch

There is much argument about the best way of disposing of waste. Apart from persuading people to reduce consumption, the two main methods of getting rid of our rubbish is to bury it at landfill sites or to burn it (known as incineration). Some environmentalists say that incineration produces smoke and ash that contains hazardous chemicals, and that it discourages recycling. Other commentators believe it is the best option for reducing the waste mountain.

66 If developed countries want to reduce the waste that goes to landfill, rather than simply make green gestures, incineration ... is the best way to do it. 99 The Economist

However, some very poor people use rubbish to provide them with the things they need. In New York, people hunt through litter bins to find bottles and drink cans to recycle for cash. Indeed, recycling and reusing materials has become

▲ *Solid waste, such as household rubbish, is set to increase 4 or 5 times by 2025. Here waste is being buried in a landfill site, but some areas in the UK have run out of suitable locations.*

◀ *A rubbish collector in Cairo, Egypt. The rubbish collectors make a living by sorting and recycling everything from aluminium to textiles and paper.*

increasingly popular in recent times. Bottle and paper banks are now a common sight in some countries. There has even been talk of British county councils mining landfill sites for reusable materials such as plastics and glass. Individuals can also do their bit to help. For example, Peter Harper, who works at the Centre for Alternative Technology in Wales, is so keen on recycling that he turns all his kitchen waste into compost. He has also done up the terraced stone cottage where he lives – but not as most people would. He refused to have skips or bonfires and made sure that everything he took out of his house was reused.

But although aluminium drink cans can be recycled over and over again and still look the same, other materials such as glass, plastics, steel and paper lose some quality when they are recycled. Another problem is that recycling uses up a lot of energy which can add to the problems of pollution and global warming.

▲ *Nearly everything can be recycled – including bottles. But will recycling solve the problem of waste or should we be looking at reducing the amount of waste in the first place?*

▼ *This picture shows huge blocks of crushed aluminium cans ready to be recycled.*

" At some point recycling will cease to save energy at all ... so long as it is powered by fossil or nuclear fuels it will start making a net contribution to pollution. "
Michael Jacobs,
The Green Economy

Recycling can also be time-consuming as items to be recycled have to be collected and separated. Some people think that buying recycled products makes shoppers complacent and that problems with the environment run far deeper. They believe that the richer countries should be making more effort to reduce consumption and therefore waste.

" With a new baseball season under way, fans will once again enjoy their peanuts and crackerjack... A single hot dog wrapper might not seem much, but multiply it by the 26 million frankfurters consumed at major league baseball stadiums in 2002, add all the other junk generated by 68 million fans, and you'll get enough trash – about 43 million tons – to, well...fill a stadium. " Ron Kaplan, The Environmental Magazine

However, little money appears to be going into the reduction of waste.

" Over 99 per cent of US Federal and State environmental spending is devoted to controlling pollution after waste is generated. Less than one per cent is spent to reduce the generation of waste. "
US Congress Office of Technology Assessment

Rich versus poor?

The growing gap between the rich and poor people of the world is one of the biggest problems we face today. Just 358 of the world's richest people, all billionaires, have the same amount of money as 2,750 million other people. There are more than 1.1 billion people in poverty, most of them living in developing countries in Asia and Africa.

Whilst reading this book, you may have noticed that differences of opinion between rich and poor countries often rise to the surface when environmental issues are discussed. This is because rich and poor tend to blame each other for the dilemma the world is in. Richer countries often view the 'backward' methods of developing countries as a barrier to sustainable development. Many of those who live in developing countries, on the other hand, feel that they have been forced into their present position by the actions of those industrialized nations in the past.

▶ *The logging industry is financially very important for many countries in the developing world. However, logging can also spoil the land available for farming and water supplies and leave fewer places to hunt or gather traditional medicines.*

Part of the problem is that because of colonialism many developing countries are now in a dependent state, their nature has been stripped bare and they were paid miserably for the destruction of their natural resources. Now the former colonists owe a kind of debt.
Martin Khor Kok Peng, Director, Third World Network, Malaysia

The 1992 Earth Summit in Rio, Brazil was called to address this problem as well as a wide range of other environmental issues. The 160 nations that attended drew up an action plan known as Agenda 21. Its key message was that the poor are very capable of using the resources they have in a sustainable manner. But it also emphasized that richer countries need to allow developing countries to compete fairly with them in the market place. National campaigns are now in place worldwide. The UK's Voluntary Local Agenda 21 involved 60 per cent of local governments in just three years.

The main aim of anti-poverty programmes is to make poor people better able to earn a living in a sustainable way. Agenda 21

One example of both rich and poor using the environment in a sustainable way that benefits both

parties is known as 'eco-tourism'. This is a type of holiday where people from richer countries visit poorer nations to see rare animals and plants. Eco-tourism has become an important income earner for developing countries like Kenya, Costa Rica, Nepal and the Maldives. Without it, they would probably be considerably poorer than they already are.

A growing number of countries are recognizing that the world's appetite for experiencing environments and cultures other than their own is a golden economic opportunity.
John Naisbitt, Global Paradox

But many people feel that developing countries will need to be treated as equal partners in all areas of business if the rich/poor divide is to be reduced.

▼ An eco-tourist watches two young mountain gorillas in Zaire.

Protest and survive?

Many people say they are worried about the environment but not everyone makes the effort to do something about it. For some, the first step is recycling newspapers and bottles, or joining a group like Friends of the Earth. Others feel so frustrated by what is happening that they protest by direct action. A wide range of people are involved in such activities.

❝ *It is not just dreadlocked travellers who care about the countryside ... it's people who are united in a world view.* ❞
The Marchioness of Worcester, who protested about a road bypass being built near Newbury

In many towns and cities around the world, such as London, Sydney and San Francisco, cyclists gather together to form a 'Critical Mass', a demonstration of tens or hundreds of riders who take over the roads in protest at our car-dominated cities. These events are called 'disorganizations' because no person or organization will claim to run them. This prevents the authorities from arresting the ringleaders or presenting them with a bill for policing costs. Although such protests are effective in that they bring the problem to the attention of a wider audience, they have also been criticized.

❝ *Direct action protests really do cause chaos, and some of the more illegal activities can cause disruption to the emergency services and people having to make urgent journeys.* ❞
AA spokesman

Some green campaigners will go as far as breaking the law during the course of their protests and many have been taken to court as a result. This can have a damaging effect for the environmental group in question.

❝ *Over the past 10 years most anti-environmental lawsuits linger in courts for an average three years, sapping the funds of activist groups and making people scared to criticize local developers for fear of being sued.* ❞ *Utne Reader, US environmental publication*

▼ *A 'Critical Mass' bicycle ride takes place through a major city centre. Are such methods effective and acceptable means of protest or do they cause more harm than good?*

because of the violent action they take. They too have been criticized because they are seen as a greater threat to society than the things they are campaigning against. However, some governments have also received criticism for the harsh tactics they have used against 'terrorists' who are actually seen as heroes by fellow environmentalists. Ken Saro-Wiwa, for example, was hanged by the Nigerian government for campaigning against the oil company Shell.

◀ Protestors clash with police over the building of a motorway extension through the countryside.

However, there have been minor victories for environmentalists. For example, the 'McLibel' case – the longest running libel case in the UK – has allowed two environmentalists to question publicly the entire McDonald's operation, from cattle ranching in Brazilian rainforests to its banning of trade unions.

Sometimes, violence is used during environmental protests. When this happens peaceful environmental groups are often the first to call for calm.

❝ We will lose public support if people see violence and criminal damage being used. ❞
Tony Juniper,
Executive Director,
Friends of the Earth

Some green campaigners are even branded 'eco-terrorists' and are seen as a national security threat

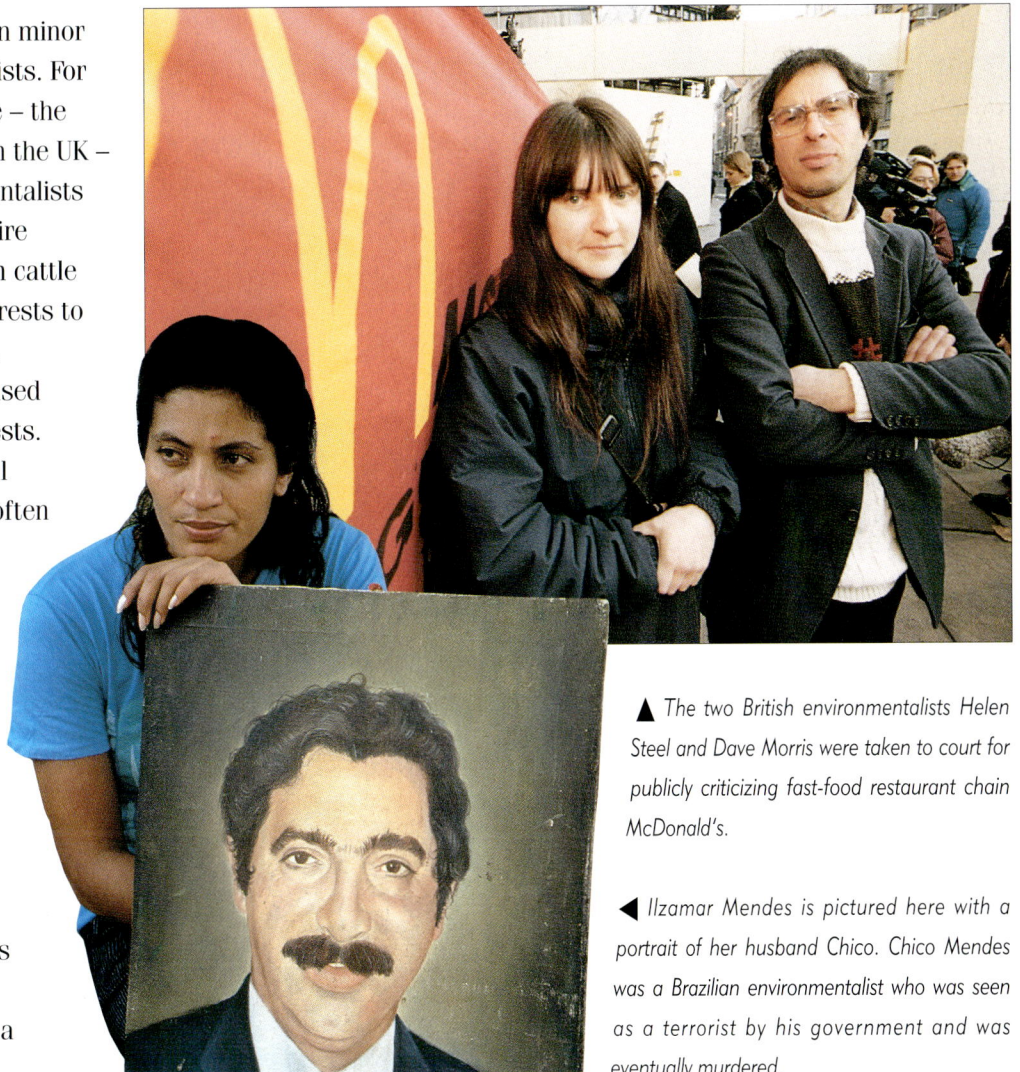

▲ The two British environmentalists Helen Steel and Dave Morris were taken to court for publicly criticizing fast-food restaurant chain McDonald's.

◀ Ilzamar Mendes is pictured here with a portrait of her husband Chico. Chico Mendes was a Brazilian environmentalist who was seen as a terrorist by his government and was eventually murdered.

A green future?

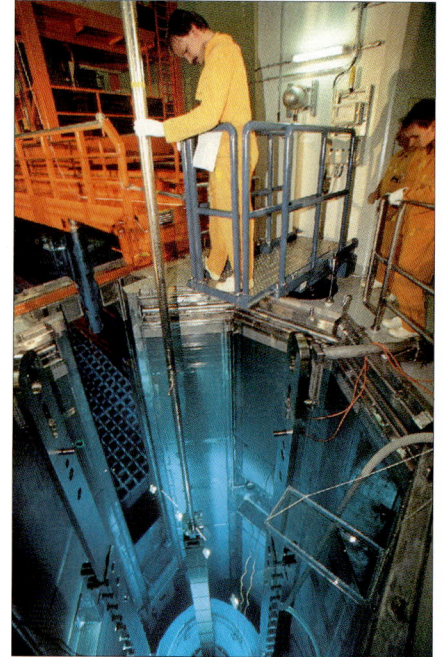

▲ Industry plays an important role in the future of our planet.

◀ A Canadian woman chopping firewood. Will we need to return to a more 'natural' way of life, such as this, to survive?

This book shows that the problems that we face concerning the environment and economic development are inter-connected.

" The planet is not arranged in national compartments. Whoever interferes with it anywhere is doing something that is of serious concern to the international community at large. "
George Kennan, Foreign Affairs

It therefore follows that, if we want sustainable development, we will have to think of solving our problems on an international, rather than just a local scale. However, one of the main problems with this is the widening gap between the richer and poorer nations. In poorer countries there are not enough resources to sustain their ever-growing populations. In richer countries there are too many people living unsustainable lifestyles because they

rely on fossil fuels, which may run out, cause pollution and add to global warming. But is it unfair to stop the poor using their resources to develop in the same way?

" One of the key features of any corporate accountability framework must be the protection of communities' control over their own resources and ability to address poor social and environmental conditions. " Friends of the Earth

And although some measures have been imposed in Western nations to regulate the environment they are seen by some as being superficial and hypocritical.

66 The white man's laws don't make sense. There are laws to protect eagles, yet their nesting sites are cut down. There are laws to protect salmon, yet their spawning grounds are disturbed. There are laws to protect indigenous people, yet their homelands and village sites are destroyed and they are removed from the land. 99
Nuxalk elder, Canada

Another problem with sustainable development is many businesses, especially in the power and construction industries, are not always environmentally friendly. Many blame them for the problems we now face.

66 The causes of environmental damage lie in economic activities – in agricultural and industrial production, in the consumption of energy and the discharge of wastes.... To the naïve observer it might then appear obvious that, if the crisis is to be tackled, economic policy must be changed. 99
Michael Jacobs, The Green Economy

But the sheer size and importance of these companies is the reason why some people think we should be putting more effort into persuading them of the viability of sustainable development. This, however, can be a difficult task if businesses are not fully behind the idea.

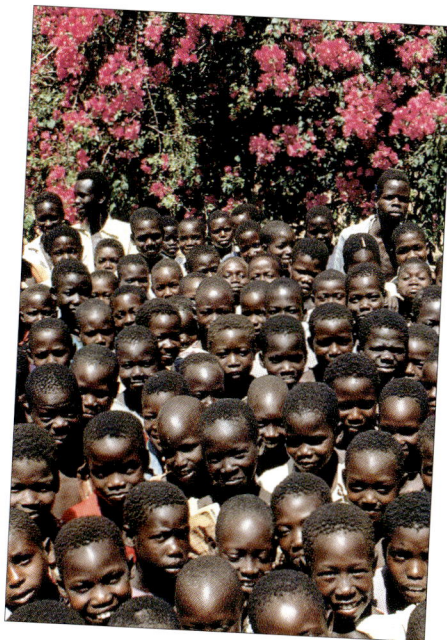

66 In a perfect world preserving any country's natural resources would be supported globally for the greater good. But this is not a perfect world. All too often protecting natural resources means sacrificing jobs, economic opportunity and local customs. 99
John Naisbitt, Global Paradox

◀ Will future generations be able to live in a more environmentally friendly world?

The challenge of sustainable development is ensuring that our children and children's children – the world's future generations – will be living in a fairer, greener world. The route may not yet be clear, but many people feel we must find a way.

66 The gross imbalances that have been created by concentration of economic growth in the industrial countries and population growth in the developing countries is at the centre of the current dilemma. Sorting this out will be the key to our future – in environmental and economic as well as traditional security terms. 99 Maurice Strong, United Nations Commission on Environment and Development

▼ Will sites of natural beauty be destroyed if we do not achieve sustainable development?

Glossary

ACID RAIN Rain which contains chemicals from industrial pollution, like sulphur dioxide and nitrogen oxides. Acid rain can kill plants and trees, and damage buildings.

AGRICULTURE Another word for farming.

ATMOSPHERE The layer of air which surrounds the Earth.

BIODIVERSITY Describes the wealth of species in the world.

CLIMATE The weather and temperatures associated with different areas on the Earth's surface.

CONSUMERISM The buying of goods. Consumerism is often associated with richer Western countries whose people buy a comparatively large amount of goods.

DEVELOPED COUNTRIES Richer countries which rely on industry (for example, the UK, the USA and Japan).

DEVELOPING COUNTRIES Poorer countries which are trying to industrialize (like many in Africa, South America and South-east Asia). Also known as third world countries.

ECONOMIC DEVELOPMENT The growth in size and profits of businesses.

ENVIRONMENTALIST A person who is concerned about and wants to protect the environment.

FERTILIZERS Chemicals used on farming land to help crops grow.

FOSSIL FUELS Fuels, such as oil, gas and coal which are made from fossilized substances. Once used they cannot be replaced, so they are also known as non-renewable resources.

GLOBAL WARMING The warming of the atmosphere which also causes the surface of the Earth to heat up. Many scientists believe global warming is caused by greenhouse gases.

GREENHOUSE EFFECT Natural process which traps warm air around the Earth's surface, in a similar way to glass in a greenhouse, making it warm enough for life.

GREENHOUSE GASES Gases which many people believe disturb the greenhouse effect and increase global warming. Includes CFCs (chloro-fluorocarbons) and CO_2 (carbon dioxide).

HABITAT A place where a particular group of plants or animals live.

HUMAN RIGHTS The rights to freedom and equality that many people believe every human being should have.

INDIGENOUS People, plants or animals which have lived in an area for hundreds or thousands of years.

OZONE LAYER A protective 'shield' of gas which stops harmful ultraviolet rays from the Sun passing through the Earth's atmosphere.

PESTICIDE A chemical used on crops to kill insects and pests.

POLLUTION The damaging of the environment by man-made gases, chemicals and waste.

SUSTAINABLE DEVELOPMENT Economic development which meets the needs of the present generation without spoiling the environment for future generations.

ULTRAVIOLET RAYS (UV rays) Harmful rays from the Sun which can cause skin cancer.

UNSUSTAINABLE DEVELOPMENT Economic development which may damage the environment.

Useful addresses

UK

Nuclear Industry Association
First floor, Whitehall House
41 Whitehall, London SW1A 2BY
www.niauk.org

British Wind Energy Association
Renewable Energy House
1 Aztec Row, Berneys Road
London N1 0PW
www.bwea.co.uk

Friends of the Earth
26-28 Underwood Street
London N1 7JQ
www.foe.co.uk

Greenpeace
Canonbury Villas
London N1 2PN
www.greenpeace.org.uk

Sustain: the alliance for better food
and farming
94 White Lion Street
London N1 9PF
www.sustainweb.org

WWF-UK
Panda House
Weyside Park
Godalming
Surrey GU7 1XR
www.wwf-uk.org

Australia

Greenpeace Australia Pacific
Level 4
35-39 Liverpool Street
Sydney NSW 2000
www.greenpeace.org.au

The Wilderness Society
57E Brisbane Street
Hobart TAS 7000
www.wilderness.org.au

WWF Australia
PO Box 528
Sydney NSW 2001
www.wwf.org.au

Facts to think about

◆ 80 million new mouths need to be fed each year. Most of them are in the developing world.

◆ In the USA, 260 million tonnes of potentially dangerous waste is produced each year. England and Wales produce around 400 million tonnes of waste each year. By 2100, the UK will have half a million tonnes of radioactive waste.

◆ Two-thirds of all the chameleons in the world live on the African island of Madagascar; 99 per cent of the island's frog and toad species are found nowhere else in the world.

◆ Three billion trees are needed each year to supply enough toilet paper to wipe the bottoms of the world.

◆ It is estimated that if you were to take a thousand girls in Africa and give them one more year of primary education, they would have 500 less children. That extra year of education would cost about US$35 for each girl.

◆ Humans have destroyed more than 30 per cent of the natural world since 1970, according to WWF International.

◆ Up to 40,000 species of wildlife are estimated to become extinct each year worldwide.

◆ Atmospheric carbon dioxide is predicted to double by 2050. Many scientists believe that this could lead to a temperature rise of up to 5.8 degrees Celsius by 2100. The difference between the average temperatures of the last Ice Age (about one million years ago) and those of today is 4 °C.

Index